Simon the Bully

By Julie Haydon

Illustrations by Elise Hurst

Contents

School Bully

Simon was often angry.
Today he was very angry because his parents
had told him last night that they weren't going
to the school fair on Saturday.

They were always too busy to spend time with him.

When Ms Jackson, the teacher, wasn't looking,
Simon pushed the new boy, Tim, off his chair.

Tim fell onto the floor.

"What did you do that for?" Tim asked,
rubbing his elbow.

"Because I felt like it!" Simon said, with a nasty grin on his face.

He enjoyed hurting other kids because it made him feel important and powerful.

"Well, don't do it again," Tim said, as he picked up his book and pencils.

"Or what?" sneered Simon.

"I'll tell Ms Jackson," Tim said, calmly.

"Oh, so you're a tell-tale are you?" said Simon.

Tim stood in front of Simon and looked him in the eye. "Bullies like you don't scare me," said Tim, bravely. "So just leave me alone."

Tim moved to a different desk
and introduced himself to the children sitting there.

Some of them were looking
at Simon and laughing quietly.
"Good on you, Tim,"
said one of the boys.

Simon didn't feel quite so powerful now.
Nobody had ever stood up to him before.
He dropped his head in annoyance,
and started to do his work.

Simon

Simon is nine years old and he attends
a local primary school.
Ever since he began at the school, 12 months ago,
many children – especially the younger ones –
have been afraid of him.

The reason is that Simon is a bully.

Simon is very tall for his age
and towers over most children in his class.
Simon uses his height to frighten others.
He often frowns and scowls, too,
because he is a very unhappy person.

Simon doesn't have any friends
and is very lonely at school and at home.

His parents work long hours
so he isn't able to join a sports team.
During the weekend,
he stays with his grandmother
and watches TV or plays video games by himself.

Simon wants to go camping with his father
in the summer holidays.
He thinks they will have fun together,
because they can go fishing and hiking.
Sadly he doesn't have any friends to join them.

Simon doesn't understand
how to have fun with children his own age.
He thinks that being a bully
makes him important and powerful.

He doesn't know that having friends
is better than being a bully with no friends.